Disney
THE PRINCESS
AND THE
FROG

9
DOWN IN NEW ORLEANS

15
ALMOST THERE

23
FRIENDS ON THE OTHER SIDE

34
WHEN WE'RE HUMAN

43
GONNA TAKE YOU THERE

50
MA BELLE EVANGELINE

54
DIG A LITTLE DEEPER

65
NEVER KNEW I NEEDED

ISBN 978-1-4234-8837-8

Disney characters and artwork © Disney Enterprises, Inc.

WALT DISNEY MUSIC COMPANY

DISTRIBUTED BY

HAL•LEONARD®
CORPORATION

7777 W. BLUEMOUND RD. P.O. BOX 13819 MILWAUKEE, WI 53213

In Australia Contact:
Hal Leonard Australia Pty. Ltd.
4 Lentara Court
Cheltenham, Victoria, 3192 Australia
Email: ausadmin@halleonard.com.au

Visit Hal Leonard Online at
www.halleonard.com

DOWN IN NEW ORLEANS

Music and Lyrics by
RANDY NEWMAN

The eve-ning star is shin-ing bright, so make a wish and

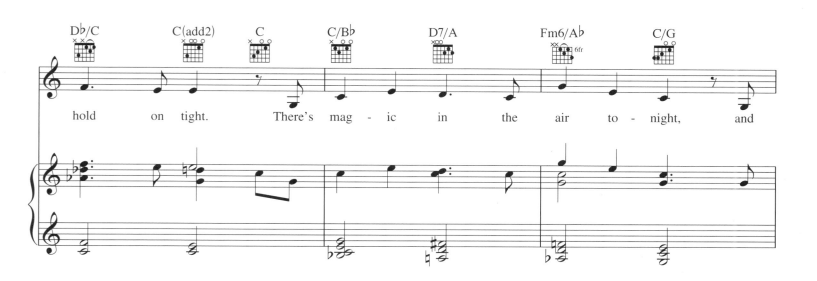

hold on tight. There's mag-ic in the air to-night, and

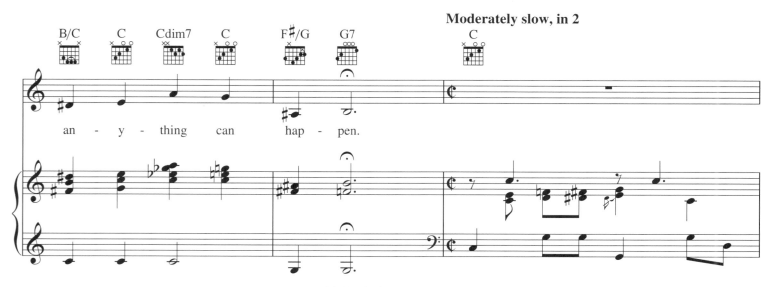

an-y-thing can hap-pen.

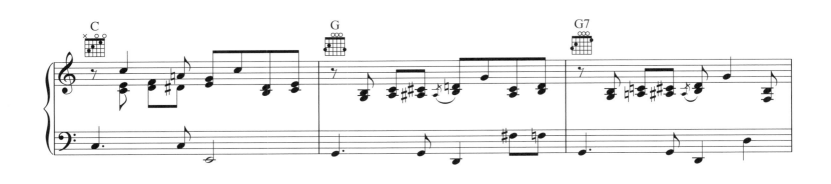

In the South - land there's a cit - y

way down____ on the riv - er,____ where the wom - en are ver -

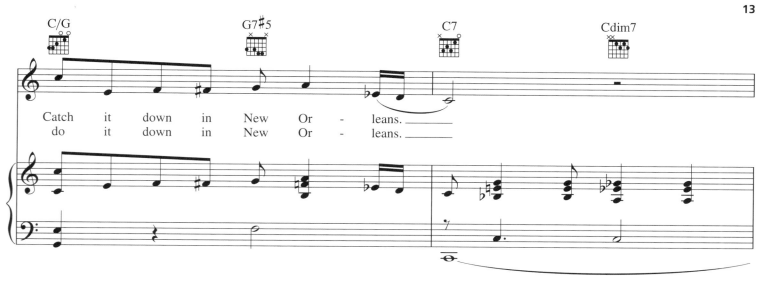

Catch it down in New Or - leans. _____
do it down in New Or - leans. _____

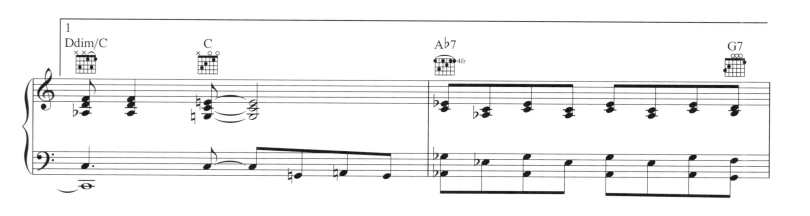

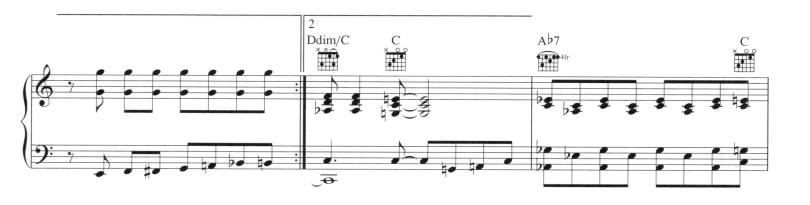

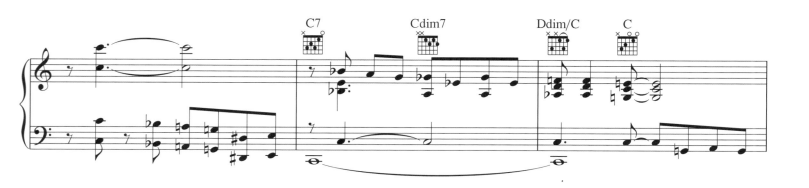

ALMOST THERE

Music and Lyrics by
RANDY NEWMAN

Moderately, expressively

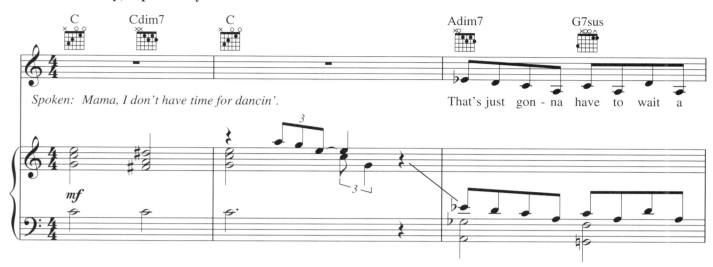

Spoken: *Mama, I don't have time for dancin'.*

That's just gon-na have to wait a

while. _ Ain't got time for mess-in' a-round, _

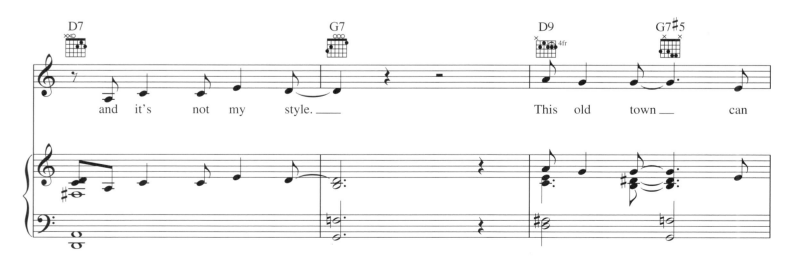

and it's not my style. ___ This old town ___ can

Peo - ple down here think I'm ___ cra - zy, but I don't care. ___ Trials ___ and trib - u - la - tions, I've had ___ my share. ___ There ain't noth - ing gon - na

stop me now ___ 'cause I'm ___ al - most there. ___

I re -

mem - ber Dad - dy told ___ me   fair - y tales can come true, _

___ but you got - ta make 'em hap - pen; it

FRIENDS ON THE OTHER SIDE

Music and Lyrics by
RANDY NEWMAN

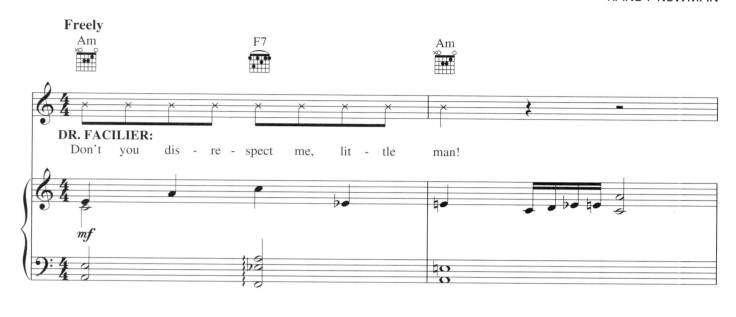

DR. FACILIER:
Don't you dis - re - spect me, lit - tle man!

Don't you der - o - gate or de - ride. You're in my world now, not

your world, and I got friends on the oth - er side.

26

28

30

WHEN WE'RE HUMAN

Music and Lyrics by
RANDY NEWMAN

as I hope to be, _____ I'm gon-na blow this horn __ 'til the

cows come home, _ and ev-'ry-one's gon-na bow down to me.

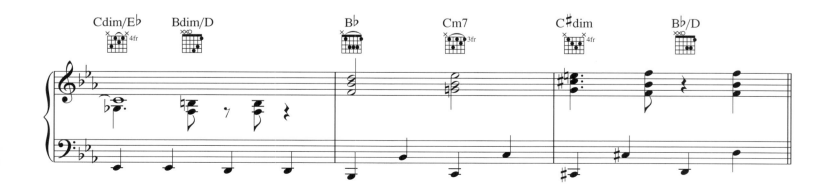

GONNA TAKE YOU THERE

Music and Lyrics by
RANDY NEWMAN

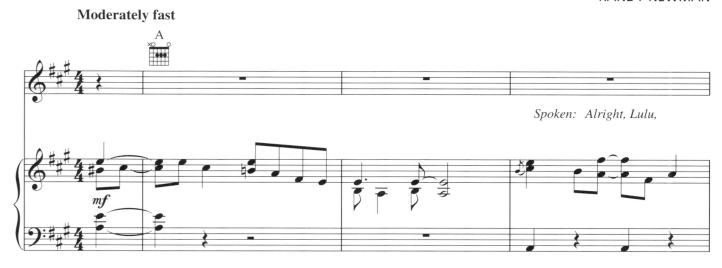

MA BELLE EVANGELINE

Music and Lyrics by
RANDY NEWMAN

DIG A LITTLE DEEPER

Music and Lyrics by
RANDY NEWMAN

Spoken: *Open up the window.*

Let in the light, children!

(Blue skies and sun - shine.)

(Blue skies and sun -

Freely

- shine.)

TIANA: Blue skies and sun - shine. _____

_____

MAMA ODIE: Guar - an - teed. (Ah!)

NEVER KNEW I NEEDED

Music and Lyrics by
SHAFFER SMITH

Moderately slow

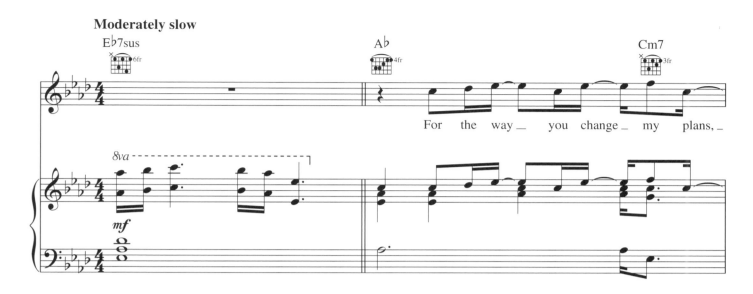

For the way __ you change __ my plans, __

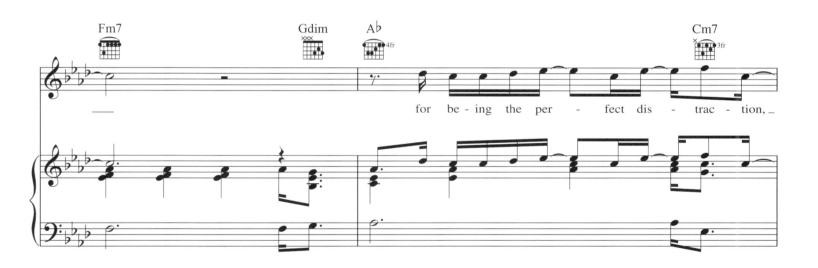

__ for be - ing the per - fect dis - trac - tion, __

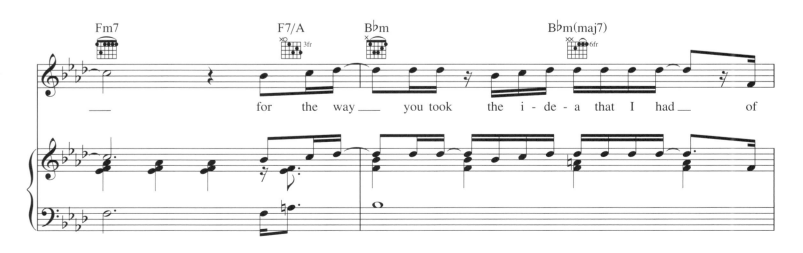

__ for the way __ you took the i - de - a that I had __ of

67